SURE SHOT

THE 100 MOST COMMON GOLF MISTAKES AND HOW TO CORRECT THEM

Gary Wiren
with Dawson Taylor

C O N T E M P O R A R Y
BOOKS, INC.
CHICAGO ▪ NEW YORK

Library of Congress Cataloging-in-Publication Data

Wiren, Gary.
 Sure shot.

 1. Golf. I. Taylor, Dawson. II. Title.
GV965.W735   1987   796.352′3   87-5298
ISBN 0-8092-5104-3 (pbk.)

Copyright © 1987 by Gary Wiren, Ph.D., and Dawson Taylor
All rights reserved
Published by Contemporary Books, Inc.
180 North Michigan Avenue, Chicago, Illinois 60601
Manufactured in the United States of America
Library of Congress Catalog Card Number: 87-5298
International Standard Book Number: 0-8092-5104-3

Published simultaneously in Canada by Beaverbooks, Ltd.
195 Allstate Parkway, Valleywood Business Park
Markham, Ontario L3R 4T8 Canada

CONTENTS

AUTHOR'S STATEMENT

Golf is a wonderful, challenging game. But it can also be a frustrating game, particularly when you continue to make mistakes and don't know how to correct them. When I hear, "I'm hitting the ball terribly and I don't have the slightest idea what to do!," it is the cry of a clearly distressed golfer who needs help.

We have all had that hopeless feeling at one time or another when perhaps a correct thought, idea, or picture could have put us straight.

That's why visually enhanced suggestions can help your game. As a teacher of golf to teachers of golf around the world, I have been privileged to work with and watch the best professionals demonstrate their skills in correcting golfers' errors. I present that information in this book in a simple and straightforward manner. If you follow the techniques I have outlined in the following pages and take the time—even if it's only for 10 minutes at a time, three sessions a week—to conscientiously practice the shots that give you the most trouble, you'll see a noticeable difference and enjoy the result.

Gary Wiren, Ph.D.
Master Teacher PGA
National Golf Club
Palm Beach Gardens, Florida
"Home of the PGA of America"

COAUTHOR'S STATEMENT

In 1983, after considerable urging, I convinced Dr. Gary Wiren to write a book about his long-driving technique and the daily exercises that help him maintain his wonderfully effective swing. That book, *Super-Power Golf*, was published in 1984 as a joint effort—Gary supplied the expert knowledge and I, the editing. *Super-Power Golf* was a resounding success.

Although long driving is of interest to most golfers, what I thought might be of help to even more golfers would be a book by Gary Wiren on error correction. Here's how it happened.

In 1969 I retired and moved to Florida to enjoy the good golfing life. I have always been a low-handicap golfer. I am 5'7" and weigh 168 pounds, and all my career I have fought the battle of the long ball. But sadly, I began losing distance and could not understand why. Age certainly was a factor; but I found myself using a 3-iron where I once used a 5-iron.

Most fortunately, at that time I attended one of the Professional Golfers' Association's instructional schools at Palm Beach Gardens, Florida. Dr. Gary Wiren conducted the week-long school. Gary discovered why I was losing distance: I was not releasing the club properly at impact. I needed a longer arc, a bigger turn, and regular exercise to strengthen my golfing muscles. With his help I recovered my game, lowering my handicap from 7 to 3; today it is at 4. Recently, I broke 70 at the Atlantis Golf Club.

This experience led to my suggestion that Gary write about golfing mistakes and how to correct them. This book is based on his work with thousands of pupils; the first-person voice through-out is his.

I sincerely hope this book will add as much to your enjoyment of golf as it has to mine.

Dawson Taylor

1
BEFORE THE SWING

Are you familiar with the golf expression, "Don't miss the shot before you swing the club"? I like it particularly because it puts proper emphasis on the preparations necessary before the swing begins.

The mechanical preparations are grip, aim, and setup. That may sound elementary, but consider making a perfect swing executed under any of the following circumstances:

1. Your grip is rotated too far clockwise and is going to return the clubface fifteen degrees open.
2. You are aiming at the water but you think you are aiming at the flag.
3. You are standing four inches too far from the ball.

In each case a perfect swing will produce a perfectly horrible shot. This is because the essential preliminaries before the swing were not properly executed.

Do not take grip, aim, and setup for granted!

Do as the PGA Tour players do: overlearn them until doing them precisely the same way each time becomes a habit. Many ordinary players may not place a high enough value on these preparatory fundamentals because the performers they see on TV handle this aspect of the game in what appears to be a casual, routine fashion. It may *look* casual, but it is very deliberate.

Consistency is one of the most sought-after goals in golf. Achieving consistency must begin with the way you place your hands on the club, where you aim your body and clubface, and where you locate the ball in relation to your stance. When you execute these steps properly, the clubface has its best chance of meeting the ball at the correct point in the swing. You will find a sample swing sequence at the end of Chapter 2.

Grip

A good definition of an effective grip is "two hands working as one." One hand should not greatly dominate the other. The tendency is for the trailing hand to dominate the lead hand or, for most golfers, for the right hand to dominate the left.* This is caused partly by the nature of the action and partly because the right hand is stronger. To assist in balancing the roles of each hand, make certain accommodations in the grip. The left-hand grip, for example, is in the palm and fingers and the right-hand grip is in the fingers only, to help equalize the dominance. The little finger of the right hand is lapped over or interlocked with the index finger of the left, not only to help the hands work as a unit, but also to take away some of the right-hand leverage action, again to balance their individual roles.

The degree of rotation of the hands in the grip is most often related to a person's ability to return the face to a square position. Weaker persons need more clockwise rotation so the V's made by the thumb and index finger of each hand point more toward the right shoulder than the chin. Physically stronger players will generally place their hands so the V's point more toward the chin than the right shoulder.

*The right-handed swing is the model in this book. Left-handers should merely translate the advice into left-handed language.

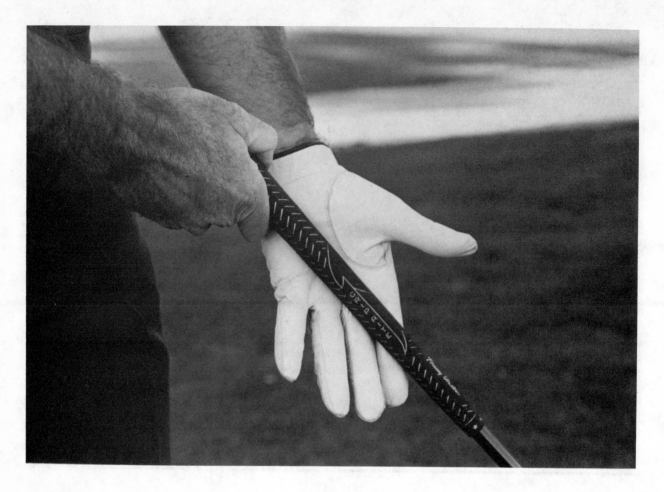

GRIP (LEFT HAND)

Mistake: The grip in the left hand should not run across the palm in this fashion. When it does, the butt end comes out above the heel pad toward the wrist, causing loss of grip control.

Correction: The grip should run more across the roots of the fingers with the butt end coming out below the heel pad of the left hand.

GRIP (LEFT HAND)

Mistake: Gripping the club with the left hand extended beyond the end also causes some loss of control of the club.

Correction: Grip the club in the left hand so that the butt end extends past the heel pad.

GRIP (RIGHT HAND)

Mistake: Gripping the club too much in the palm of the right hand, like a hammer, is a major destroyer of a swinging motion.

Correction: Place the right-hand grip in the fingers. It may not feel strong, but it produces the greatest speed and the most accuracy.

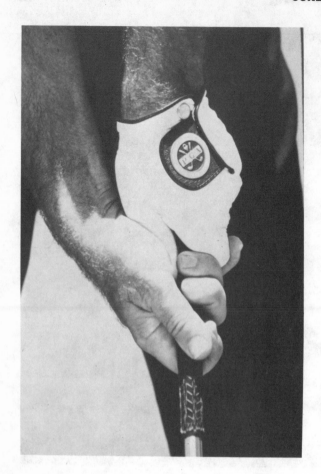 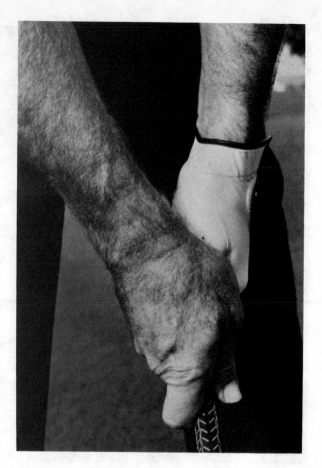

V FORMATION

Mistake: The hands are rotated too far clockwise, so the V's formed by the thumbs and index fingers point to the right of the right shoulder.

Mistake: The hands are rotated too far counterclockwise, so the V's made by the thumb and index finger of each hand point to the left of the chin.

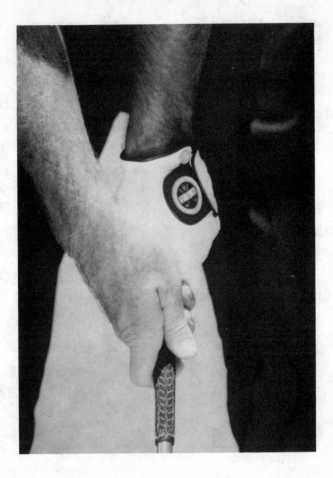

Correction: The V's of both hands should point somewhere between the right shoulder and the chin. Find your natural arm hang position when the left arm is extended and the right hand is facing the target. The right-hand grip should be in the fingers and the left-hand grip in the base of the fingers with the last three fingers in control.

OPEN FACE

CLOSED FACE

Mistake: Soling the club with the face open encourages a slice and shots that go high and to the right.

Mistake: Soling the club with the face closed encourages a hook and shots that go low and to the left.

Correction: The leading edge of the clubface should point away from you at right angles to the target.

2
THE SWING

A golf swing is exactly that—a swing. Frequently in my clinics I will hold up a club and ask what it is. The answer: "A golf club." Next I will ask, "What are you going to try to do with it?" The most frequent response: "Hit the ball."

Wrong! That's that problem—trying to *hit* the ball. You should be trying to *swing the club*.

Of course you hit the ball; but hitting implies force, and the attempt to produce force tends to create tension which destroys a swing. On the other hand, swinging with speed and accuracy has a feeling of lightness rather than tightness.

There are thousands of details to consider in attempting to swing a golf club effectively. But if you try to think your way through them during the course of a swing you won't make a swing at all. What you will make is a series of unnatural movements totally lacking the flowing blend of grace and energy that characterizes a proficient player's motion. So keep this in mind: a golf swing is made by *feel* with a certain attention to detail prior to initiating the motion. When the motion begins, rely on a mental picture or be thinking of a single swing key. But never try to think you way

through the swing ("head down, arm straight, shift my weight . . .").

How do you develop this feeling of a good golf swing? First, you must have a precise concept of your goal—a well-executed swing. A professional teacher can be an effective model and guide at this stage. Next, you must practice so that the concept becomes a feeling. That feeling is sometimes called muscle memory, which is a simple way to describe a phenomenon known as motor skill learning. This learning can be enhanced by drills selected to teach specific patterns in the swing. The practice can be hitting balls or just swinging a club, as long as you understand what you are trying to achieve.

Through practice and actually overlearning the basic mechanics of a swing, you can develop trust in the result. Then the challenges of the course and other competitors will not prevent you from doing what you know you can do. Practice alone does not make perfect; it only makes permanent. What you practice makes all the difference in the world: practice a swing, not a hit.

AN INSIDE TAKEAWAY   AN OUTSIDE TAKEAWAY

Mistake: A severe inside takeaway on the backswing encourages a reverse weight shift and looping action, causing the club to be thrown from the outside on the forward swing.

Mistake: An outside takeaway on the backswing encourages a body sway to the right, a high lifting action in the backswing, and a reverse inside loop coming forward.

Correction: Start the club back straighter away from the ball, letting the clubhead make its natural arc with the left arm as the radius.

PICKING THE CLUB UP

Mistake: Picking the club up early produces a backswing that does not properly wind the upper body. It provides only the limited power available from the hands and arms without the stronger muscles of the back and trunk.

Correction: Swinging your arms back and away from the ball allows the upper body to properly wind for greater power.

BENT ARM

Mistake: A bent left arm has allowed the backswing to be almost parallel with the ground, but the shoulders have not properly turned. The upper body is not adequately wound up, so it cannot contribute much power. The left arm also needs more extension in the backswing to get a greater arc for consistency and power.

Correction: At the top of the swing the left arm is extended but not rigid.

RAISING THE HEAD

Mistake: Raising the head so that the swing center is farther from the ball than at address makes it very difficult to consistently return the clubface squarely to the ball.

Correction: At the top of the swing, the club is parallel with the ground, the left wrist is flat, the left arm is extended but not rigid, and the head has rotated but not raised. The upper body weight is over the right leg and the left heel is slightly in the air. The back is turned to the target.

INCORRECT WEIGHT SHIFT

Mistake: This is a reverse weight shift. The upper part of the body should be over the right leg, not hanging to the left. This problem is usually caused by trying to keep the head down rather than allowing it to rotate and move slightly behind the ball. The result of the reverse weight shift is a falling back on the right foot, a bad swing path, and an early hit from the top.

Mistake: A lower body reverse-weight shift results in a very weak position to swing the club aggressively. When the lower body is in a reversed position on the backswing, the weight tends to go back to the right in the downswing, which, of course, is the wrong direction. The lower and upper body weight should be over the right leg, not reversed backward over the left.

CORRECT WEIGHT SHIFT

Correction: Look again at the photo on page 27 and note that the upper body weight is more over the right leg. One way to correct a reverse weight shift and improve weight transfer is to practice raising the left leg in the air during the backswing. . . .

Correction: . . . then swinging forward until the right leg leaves the ground. Let the arms hang naturally, grip lightly, and let the momentum of the weight shift provide the power rather than trying to hit with the arms and hands.

INSIDE SWING

OUTSIDE SWING

Mistake: Crossing the flight line at the top of the swing with a raised right elbow and a cupped left wrist not only causes the club to point to the right of the target but also encourages a forward swing that is too far to the inside. The result is a push slice or a possible sweeping hook, depending on the face position.

Mistake: Laying the club off so that it points to the left of the target at the top of the swing with a flat wrist and closed clubface encourages a swing from outside of the flight line and results in a pulled hook or possible slice, depending on the face position.

Correction: At the top of the swing the club is nearly parallel with the target line. Shorter irons may not be quite parallel; the driver may go slightly past.

LOSS OF CLUB CONTROL

Mistake: Relaxing the last three fingers of your left hand at the top of the backswing causes you to lose control.

Correction: Hold snugly with those last three fingers without squeezing too tightly.

ARCHED WRIST

CUPPED WRIST

Mistake: The left wrist is arched in this position, known as *laying the club off* (see "Outside Swing" photo, page 32). It closes the clubface at the top of the swing and encourages a hook.

Mistake: The left wrist is one of the controlling factors in the clubface position at the top of the swing. Here the cupped wrist produces an open clubface (toe pointed to the ground) and encourages a slice.

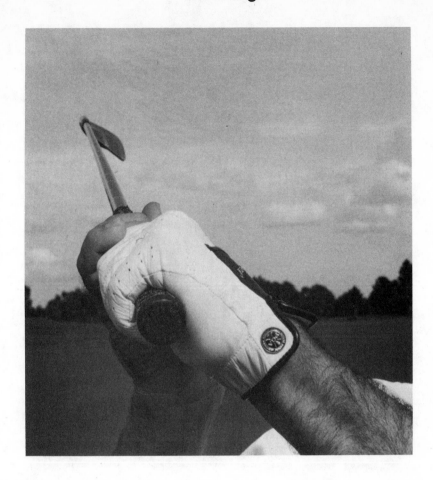

Correction: The left wrist at the top of the swing in a natural position that produces the most consistent results is one that's in a plane with the back of the arm. From this position it is much easier to return to the ball with the face square.

TOO MUCH LATERAL LEAD

Mistake: Too much lateral lead with the lower body will drop the club on an exaggerated inside-to-outside path, resulting in a push, push slice, or wide hook.

Correction: Here the body is properly aligned.

CROWDING THE BALL

Mistake: Crowding the shot will make you either hit behind the ball or cause you to bend your arms at impact and lose clubhead speed.

REACHING FOR THE BALL

Mistake: Reaching for the ball produces an erratic swing path, poor balance, and shots that go both left and right.

THE SETUP

Correction: After taking a grip, bring your arms down until you feel pressure on your chest and bend forward at the hips, soling the club. . . .

Correction: . . . Then adjust your feet.

THE ADDRESS

Mistake: The hands are too far back and the feet too wide, causing the head to be behind the ball and the weight too far to the right.

Addressing with an Iron

Addressing with a Wood

Correction: In the proper address position for the short iron, the hands will lead the clubhead at address and the head will be more over the ball than behind it. (Note: the camera position is at a slight angle that makes the ball appear farther back in the stance than it actually is.)

Correction: A good address position for the tee shot is with the ball played somewhere between the left shoulder and the left ear. The left arm and club are an extension from the left shoulder, and the right arm hangs in a natural address position. The upper body weight is slightly behind the ball, perhaps 60 percent to the right, 40 percent to the left. The lower body weight is more evenly balanced. The shoulders are parallel to the flight line.

SHANKING THE BALL

Mistake: When the ball contacts the hosel of an iron club from an outside-to-in swing path the result is a shank.

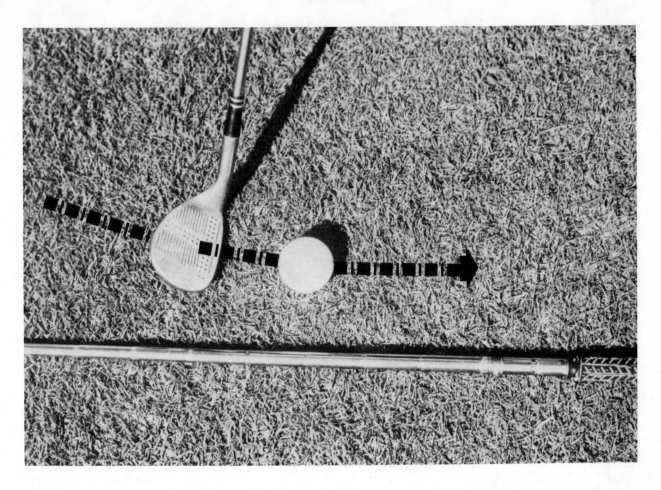

Correction: Swinging on a path that approaches the ball from slightly inside will put the center of the clubface on the ball. Do this by swinging the arms rather than throwing with the hands. This is true for both the irons and the woods.

AIMING TO THE LEFT

Mistake: Aiming too far to the left encourages the swing to go in that direction, cutting across the target line, and producing a slice or a pull shot.

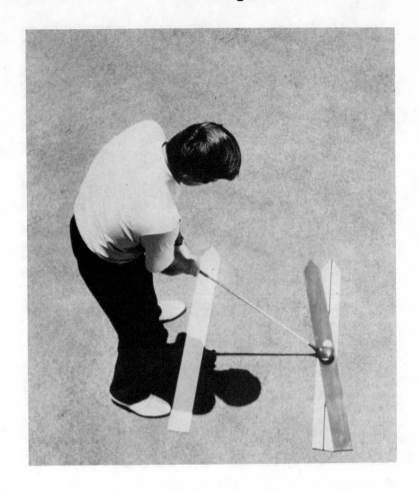

Mistake: Aiming too far to the left (view from above).

AIMING TO THE RIGHT

Mistake: Aiming too far to the right encourages a pushed shot. Hitting shots to the right causes pulling across the line to try to bring the ball back to the center. Generally, the result is a slice.

Mistake: Aiming to the right (view from above).

THE POWER PATH

Correction: This is the power path in golf, the swing that comes from the inside of the target line to the ball, down the target line, and back to the inside again. The body is properly aligned; also, the left wrist is solid at impact, rather than collapsed and cupped as is so often the case when it is overpowered by the right side.

IMPACT POSITION

Correction: The correct path is from the inside, but the correct impact position looks like this. There is only one moment of truth in the golf swing—impact, when the clubface meets the ball. Here I'm using an Impact Bag* to teach the correct feeling.

The back of the left wrist is flat, not broken down, and the right hand has not passed the left. This practice aid is the best I've ever used for transmitting the feeling of this critical position. I strongly recommend it.

---

*Impact Bag is available from Golf Works,
4820 Jackson Town Road, State Route 13,
Newark, Ohio 43055.

THE FULL SWING

Here is the full swing sequence for a fairway wood:

Backswing

Address the ball left of center between the left ear and shoulder.

Start the club away by a push, keeping your left arm extended, supported by the right hand.

Top of the Swing

Just past the right hip the hands begin to cock so that by the time the left arm is horizontal the club will be nearly vertical.

At the top of the backswing, the club is nearly parallel with the ground and the left arm is still extended though not necessarily straight. The upper body weight is over the right leg. The back slopes away from the target and the left wrist is flat.

Downswing

In the beginning of the downswing, the weight shifts over to the left side, the hands and arms drop from the over-the-shoulder position to one that comes from the inside, the wrist is still cocked, and the nearly 90-degree angle of left arm and club shaft is maintained.

The right elbow comes to the pocket as the left hip clears out of the way so the arms can swing aggressively through the shot.

Impact and Follow-Through

At impact the arms are extended and the left wrist is flat.

Halfway into the follow-through, the left elbow has begun to fold, allowing the left hand to rotate and the right arm to extend in a "shaking hands" position. The last three fingers of the left hand are still holding on.

The Finish

Swing to a good finish—in balance, club behind the head, arms comfortable and over the shoulder, weight fully to the left.

3
AROUND THE GREEN

The best golfers in the world do not hit all eighteen greens in regulation figures; most golfers hit fewer than a third of them during a round. That means there are lots of opportunities for those little shots around the green—the chip, the pitch, and the bunker shot. Working on these three skills, combined with improved putting, will lower your score faster than any other investment of your practice time.

Whenever we hit a golf shot, even short shots around the green, there is a tendency to tighten and hit *to* the ball rather than through it. A true swing will not slow as it approaches the ball and stop abruptly at contact. A swinging motion in a short shot should have acceleration through the shot and a follow-through of approximately the same length as that of the backstroke—a movement not unlike that of a playground swing.

In a badly executed short shot, the player either makes a backswing that is too long and tries to decelerate or swings too short and rushes to hit harder.

One difference between the short-game swing and the full swing is in the grip position. For a chip or short pitch, when very little velocity is needed, the hands should be placed lower on the shaft; this provides better control. This type of shot is made with little or no wrist cock in the backswing. The motion is more like a pendulum stroke, as in putting.

As the length of the shot begins to exceed that of a short chip or pitch, gradually add wrist cock for greater speed without greater effort. A swing with the wrists cocked is often called a *two-lever swing*; a shorter shot like the chip or putt is called a *one-lever swing*.

The proper setup is as important as

the proper swing in the bunker shot. The swing is almost always a two-lever swing with the wrists cocking more abruptly than usual. The shot from the sand with the ball sitting on top does not differ a great deal from a pitch shot from the grass over a bunker. The major change is the ball position. The ball should be played more forward in the stance in order to hit the sand and not the ball. Remember not to just hit the sand and stop. Finish your swing the way you see it illustrated in the photographs in this chapter.

Developing your short game will add confidence to your longer shots, since the consequence of missing a green diminish when you are confident that you can get the ball up and down in two strokes.

Chipping and Pitching

The chip and pitch shots are miniature swings with an altered body position at address. Selecting the proper club enhances your chance of hitting a good shot. It takes greater skill to play a more lofted club because the margin of error is smaller if you mis-hit the shot. A good rule to follow is to run the ball when you can, loft it when you have to.

Remember in playing pitches and chips that the loft is built into the club. You should never feel that you have to lift the shot, only that you need to get the clubface on the ball. So choose the correct club, set up so that the club will be descending on the ball, and swing forward.

Another difference that is critical for successful short shots is the setup. For all chip shots, the centerline of the body running from your nose downward should be ahead, to the left of the ball in the address. The hands are in line with the left thigh and the ball in the center of your stance. This setup encourages a slight descent on the forward swing, which assures that the ball will get on the center of the clubface. In the chip the feet are closer together than in a full shot, with the left foot drawn back to open the body more to the target. The open stance position allows the backswing to be more on the target line rather than being taken inside.

TOO MUCH LOFT

Mistake: The most frequent chipping error is selecting a club with too much loft when loft is not needed. Here, for example, the selected club is a wedge.

Correction: Use a more straight-bladed club, in this case a 6-iron, and stroke the ball like a putt but with descent.

SETUP MIS-HITS

Mistake: Trying to chip with the hands centered and the head behind the ball guarantees mis-hit shots.

Correction: Playing the shot with the hands ahead of the ball and the head over it or slightly ahead will improve your consistency.

SCOOPING THE BALL

Mistake: Attempting to lift the shot by scooping the ball in the air is the most common cause of hitting behind a pitch shot or blading the ball across the green.

Correction: Let the arms swing, keeping the hands ahead of the clubhead. Instead of trying to lift the ball, let the clubhead descend so the loft in the clubface can lift it.

THE PITCH FROM HEAVY ROUGH

Mistake: Trying to pitch the ball from heavy rough with a normal swing results in too much grass between the blade and the ball.

Correction: Make a steeper backswing when the ball is down in the heavy rough, so that the angle of descent will be greater and the clubface will not catch up in the grass. Use a sand wedge for this shot.

Bunker Shot

Playing a shot from a sand bunker is one of the hardest shots in golf when you don't know how and one of the easiest when you do know how. First, play the shot with the club made specifically for that situation, the sand wedge.

The execution of the shot is very similar to that of a pitch with these small adjustments:

1. Move the ball forward in your stance so the club strikes the sand and not the ball.

2. Cock your wrists more abruptly so that you'll get more descent.

3. Open the clubface slightly to help guarantee bounce and to avoid digging from the sole of the club.

4. Let the swing travel to the left of your target so that you are hitting a cut shot.

A brief practice session in the bunker working on the correct mechanics can quickly reduce any fear of sand.

SLIDING

Mistake: The feet are not dug into the sand. With any effort in the swing the feet will not hold their position. This can cause the player to slide and mis-hit the shot.

Correction: Work the feet down into the sand to get a more stable base.

HANDS BEHIND THE BALL

Mistake: Setting the hands behind the ball encourages the player to level out the swing at the bottom too quickly and bounce the club off the sand into the ball rather than beneath it.

Correction: The hands should be in a normal pitch-shot position slightly ahead of the ball. This will improve the angle of attack, provide a more descending blow, and cut the sand from underneath the ball.

But when the ball is sitting on top of the sand, it should be played forward in the stance off the left heel as in the picture on the right. The club should strike two to three inches behind the ball and cut a slice of sand from underneath it.

BURIED LIE

If the ball is buried, however, there should be a different set-up.

Correction: Place the ball slightly farther back toward the right in the stance so that the hands are advanced ahead of the clubhead. Do not open the blade but allow the leading edge to turn downward so it will dig rather than bounce. Allow for considerably more roll.

THE CHIP SHOT

Mistake: A chip shot out of a bunker is a very difficult shot to play.

Correction: A full swing generally makes a bunker shot much easier.

DECELERATION

Mistake: Decelerating near impact is one of the most common mistakes in bunker play and causes the ball to stay in the bunker.

Correction: Swing the club to a more full finish with the weight moving from the right foot and to the left. The length of the follow-through should be at least equal to that of the backswing. Obviously, in a short bunker shot the follow-through will not be as extended.

SHORT LOW BACKSWING

Mistake: A backswing that is too low and too short will not allow the clubhead to descend properly with enough acceleration. The result will be a lifting action that strikes the ball without taking enough sand (sometimes none at all) and blades the ball out of the bunker and across the green.

Correction: The wrist should cock more quickly than normal in the takeaway to get the club up in the backswing where it can make a better descent on the downswing.

UPHILL LIE

Mistake: Some uphill lies are too steep to match the shoulder line to the slope of the bank of sand.

Correction: Lean into the hill and hit closer behind the ball without attempting a follow-through.

DOWNHILL LIE

Mistake: In a downhill bunker shot the tendency is to hit too far behind the ball and sail it across the green. This usually happens because the shoulder line is tilted upward and the ground is tilted downward.

Correction: Tilt the shoulders to conform to the level of the ground so that the club will follow its slope down and through, cutting the sand from underneath the ball. If both feet are in the bunker, the shot should be played a little more toward the right foot in the stance.

USING A WOOD FROM THE SAND

Mistake: Playing a fairway wood from a bunker is difficult; it is almost impossible if the ball is in a poor lie.

Correction: If the ball is sitting up perfectly on top of the sand, a lofted wood can be used. But if a lip obstructs the shot, pitch out safely with a more lofted club.

FAIRWAY BUNKER SHOT

Correction: On a full iron shot from a fairway bunker, choke down on the club and play the ball back in your stance in order to contact the ball first, not the sand.

4
PUTTING

Willie Park, Jr., a famous nineteenth-century Scottish golfer, once said, "The man who can putt is a match for anyone." And he was right.

Once you have established your long game, putting well will result in a great many stroke savers, par savers, or even bogey savers.

Putting is almost a game unto itself. No other aspect of golf invites such a diversity of individual styles while at the same time requiring such precise execution.

Although variations in equipment and style are more the norm than the exception, a putt is still a swing. Grip lightly, feel the weight of the clubhead, and accelerate *through*, not *to*, the ball. Develop a comfortable routine and repeat it on each putt. This will ingrain a pattern, build confidence, and reduce tension.

- Stand bent forward at the hips so that the left eye is over the ball. This places the body the correct distance away from the ball so that the natural swing arc of the putter will be neither too far inside your target line nor too far out. In this setup, the ball is also far enough forward so that it is stroked at the bottom of the swing arc or just as the arc is coming up.

- Be positive. The greatest golfers I've ever seen are all supremely confident in their putting ability.

- Visualize the ball rolling across the green toward the target before you hit it; feel the stroke and trust the feeling.

HANDS TOO FAR AHEAD OF THE CLUB

Mistake: Advancing your hands too far ahead of the clubhead hoods the face and drives the ball down into the turf, making it hop before it rolls.

Correction: A good standard ball placement is under the left eye near the inside of the left heel. Let your hands hang naturally, only slightly ahead of the clubhead.

HITTING RIGHT OF THE HOLE

HITTING LEFT OF THE HOLE

Mistake: Taking the putter blade too far to the inside early in the backswing encourages a return on that same path, causing the ball to go to the right.

Mistake: Taking the putter blade too far to the outside encourages a return of the face so that the ball goes to the left of target.

Correction: Taking the blade back down the line for the first few inches makes it easier to return the blade squarely to the target. As the backswing continues, the putter should eventually come inside of the straight line in a natural arc.

PULLING THE BALL LEFT   PUSHING THE BALL RIGHT

Mistake: Proper alignment is one of golf's most difficult fundamentals and is particularly important for accurate putting. Here the body alignment is to the left and encourages the player to pull the ball unless he or she compensates by blocking out the release and pushing the blade toward the target.

Mistake: The alignment is now too far to the right, so the player must pull the swing back toward the hole and cut across the line of flight in order to keep the ball on the correct path.

Correction: Keep the shoulders and feet parallel to the target line. To help with distance on a downhill putt, imagine that the cup is closer (at the white circle). On an uphill putt, picture the cup to be farther than it actually is.

TOO LONG OF A BACKSTROKE

Mistake: A backswing that is too long causes the putter head to decelerate as it approaches the ball. This is one of the most common putting mistakes and produces very erratic results.

Correction: A shorter backstroke with positive acceleration rolls the ball much more consistently. The backswing, however, should not be so short that the putting motion feels like hitting rather than stroking.

READING THE GREENS

Reading greens successfully requires an ability to recognize whether grain will be a factor. Bermuda grass greens have a thicker blade and more grain. Brushing the putter left to right against the grain of this Bermuda green brings up a nap. Putting against the grain requires more effort in the stroke; with the grain, less. You are not allowed to test the green in this manner during play.

Finding the right putter in the first place is sometimes a lifelong search. A good putter can make a big difference, so select one with care.

5

THE MOST COMMON ERRORS

There are certain mistakes in trying to hit a golf ball that are made more frequently than others—golf's most common errors. For some players, these problems are perennial; they repeat them over and over, year after year, without ever doing anything substantial to make a change. Yet all problems in golf have solutions—some of which are quite simple. Identifying the cause of the error is the first step toward correction, and that step is then followed by the application of the correct solution. The examples in this chapter may help you to eliminate a particular mistake that is frequent enough in your play to be considered a perennial problem.

TOPPING THE BALL

Mistake: Topping the ball is caused by hitting it above its center. In this case the head and center of the swing have raised up from their original position at address.

Mistake: The head and the center of the swing have moved back to the right as a result of trying to lift the ball into the air. If the weight stays on the back foot during the forward swing, the club reaches the bottom of the arc too soon and tops the ball. The first move in the forward swing should be shifting the weight to the left side.

TOPPING THE BALL

Mistake: Bending the left arm at impact raises the clubhead so the ball is topped even though the head stays down. The left arm must swing through with extension to return to the same place it was at address. Too much right-hand pressure is a frequent cause of the left arm bending.

Mistake: If the ball position is too far back in the address and the upper body moves ahead of the ball in a forward swing, the clubhead will not have reached the bottom of the arc and will catch the ball on top.

TOPPING THE BALL

Mistake: The ball positioned too far forward is a far more common cause of topping, however, than the ball played too far back.

Correction: Here the head, center of the swing, and left arm are in their proper positions for correct ball contact.

INCORRECT BALL IMPACT

Mistake: Impacting the ball in the heel of the clubface results in a fade and lost distance. Usually this is caused by hitting too early with the hands in the forward swing and casting the clubhead path outside of the flight line.

Mistake: Impacting the ball on the toe will create a toe hook and lost distance. This is usually caused by tension in the arms that pulls the club inward.

HITTING BEHIND THE BALL

Mistake: Hitting behind the ball—a fat shot—is the result of the clubhead arriving out of sequence, before the weight shift to the left side and the forward arm swing have been completed.

Mistake: Lowering your body substantially from its original starting point while keeping your arms extended also causes a fat shot.

HITTING BEHIND THE BALL

Mistake: Hanging back on the right side causes the fat shot.

Correction: The weight should shift to the left toward the target, allowing the right heel to release.

CORRECTING THE FAT SHOT

Correction: On the full swing, the release of the right foot is even more complete—the heel to toe line is vertical—and the divot comes out after the ball has been struck first. Here a tee has been placed in the ground to show where the ball's location had been. Note the divot ahead.

Correction: Here is a drill to help correct the fat shot. In this short-iron setup, the ball is played correctly slightly left of center with the hands ahead of the clubhead.

When the weight transfer leads the swing to the left side, a divot will come out ahead, starting at the tee and continuing ahead of it.

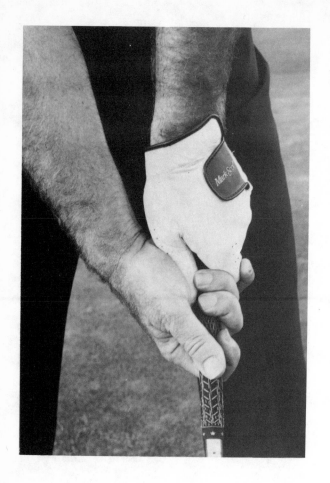

COMMON ERRORS THAT CAUSE YOU TO HOOK THE BALL

Mistake: The grip is too strong.

Mistake: The ball is back in the stance and the shoulders closed.

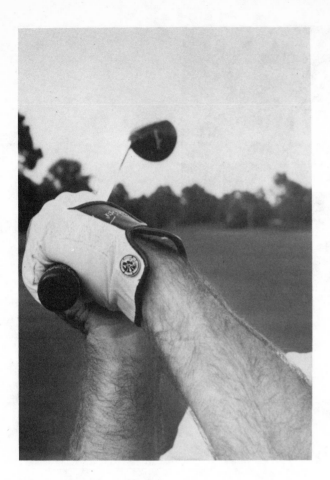

Mistake:　The face is shut.

Mistake:　The weight is back on the right foot.

Mistake: Rolling the forearms with a closed clubface.

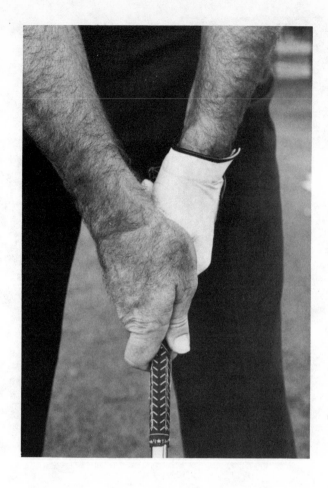

COMMON ERRORS THAT CAUSE YOU TO SLICE THE BALL

Mistake: The grip is too weak.

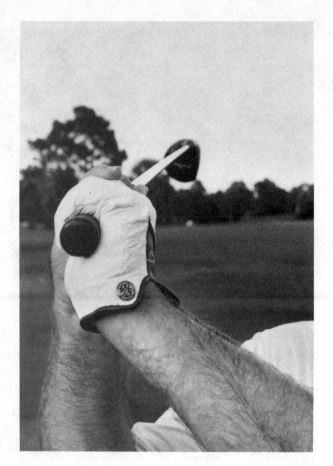

Mistake: The ball is forward in the stance and the shoulders open.

Mistake: The clubface is open.

Mistake: The weight is too far left.

Mistake: Blocking with an open face.

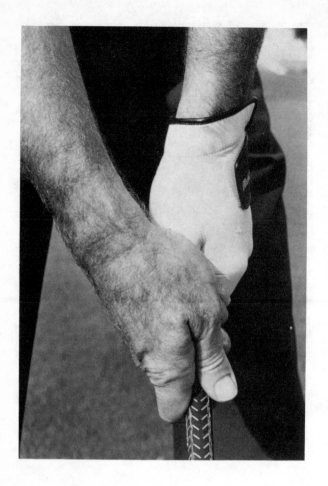 

CORRECTING THE HOOK AND THE SLICE

Correction: Start with a good grip.

Correction: The takeaway is square.

Correction: The wrist is flat at the top and the club parallel to the flight line.

Correction: Impact is with weight to the left and back of the left hand toward the target.

Correction: Finish totally left—arms are comfortable and the upper body is released toward the target.

6

UNUSUAL LIES AND CONDITIONS

Golf would be a good game without unusual conditions; with them, it's a great game. Sloping lies, wet days and dry days, windy days and still days, long grass and short grass, deep sand and shallow sand, hot weather and cold weather; fast and slow, grainy and smooth, hard and soft—a golf course is never the same.

The ability to handle unusual conditions separates the star from the struggler, the champ from the chump. Study experienced golfers (including your professional) and ask them for tips on handling those out-of-the-ordinary shots.

One of the most basic principles is that whenever conditions are not normal, play more conservatively. On sloping lies, for example—above or below the feet, uphill or downhill—it is advisable to take a club that requires less effort and use a more controlled

swing. Gravity is the enemy on sloping lies. It is much more difficult to maintain balance when one foot is higher or lower than the other. On an uphill shot where the slope also increases the effective loft in your clubface, it may be necessary to use a club two or more numbers stronger, depending on the severity of the slope.

Remember also that sloping lies tend to produce different flight patterns. Shots with the ball resting above or uphill go left; below and downhill tend to go right. The easiest way to handle this is to anticipate the result and simply allow it to happen by aiming a compensating distance in the other direction.

Wind is considered a golfer's enemy. But really it's just another challenge; personally, I rather enjoy it. One thing is for sure, though: you'd better learn to hug the ground a bit more with the trajectory of your shots. Wind plays havoc with high golf shots.

The principle of trajectory control is *the more you angle the grip end forward (in advance of the clubhead), the lower the shot will travel.* Moving the grip end of the club backwards adds loft to the face and height to the trajectory. For a low shot, the standard practice is to move the ball back in the stance. When you do this, the grip end moves forward in relation to the head. To execute a shot into the wind, select a club one lower in number for the distance you wish to travel. Shorten down on your grip about two inches. Move the ball back of center in your stance and keep your hands in their normal position.

Take a three-quarter-length swing back and make a three-quarter-length finish. Don't try to punch the ball—instead just swing, keeping the relation of your hand and clubhead the same at impact as it was at address.

When attempting to increase the trajectory to go over an obstacle, move the grip end of the club back by placing the ball farther forward in the stance. Be sure to be aggressive with your weight shift and left arm or you will tend to hit a fat shot.

It takes practice to learn all of the little "tricks" or adjustments that are necessary when you face unusual lies and conditions. But doing so can save you from repeating bad shots on the course.

BALL ABOVE FEET

Mistake: When the ball is above your feet it is actually closer to you, and with a full-length grip there is a tendency to hit behind the ball. Gravity tries to move the body backward, causing you to pull the shot to the left even when the ball is hit squarely.

Correction: Shortening the grip results in a more balanced stance and the swing clears the ground better. Use a club that is stronger (lower) by one number to compensate for the loss of distance. On an uneven lie, the swing should always be slightly more controlled than under normal conditions. Aim out to the right, as the ball tends to go left.

UPHILL LIE

Mistake: On an uphill slope, gravity tugs the body back toward the rear foot and tilts the shoulder line too much. A swing from this position hits behind the ball, tops it, or pulls it strongly to the left.

Correction: Lean into the hill a bit more to fight the pull of gravity, but keep the shoulders matched with the slope of the hill and aim to the right.

BALL BELOW FEET

Mistake: When the ball is below the feet gravity tends to pull the body forward, and the tendency is to heel or shank the shot, or, because the ball is lower than normal, to top it.

Correction: Stand a little closer to the ball and sit deeply in your knees so that the weight feels more on the heels. Grip the club at the top in order to reach the ball more easily. Aim more to the left.

DOWNHILL LIE

Mistake: Do not tilt the shoulder upward and put the center of the body too far behind the ball when playing a downhill lie. A swing from this position tops the ball, hits badly behind it, or skulls the shot.

Correction: Put the shoulders in a position that matches the slope of the ground better and moves the center of the body toward the left and over the ball. This is slightly back of center, so the follow-through should be a little longer than normal.

SOLING THE CLUB IN A HAZARD

Mistake: Soling the club within the confines of a hazard is not allowed. The penalty is two strokes in medal play, loss of hole in stroke play.

Correction: Suspend the club above the ball; touch the turf only in the course of the swing.

SOLING THE CLUB IN A BUNKER

Mistake: Soling the club in this bunker is a two-stroke penalty.

Correction: Suspend the club in the air and don't brush the sand on the backswing.

COURSE ETIQUETTE

Mistake: Do not leave footprints in a bunker. It's unfair to the next player whose ball may find a bad lie due to such carelessness.

Correction: Always rake the bunker smooth.

UNPLAYABLE LIE

Mistake: The ball has landed on a cart path. Do not measure from the opposite side of the path and closer to the hole. Always find the nearest point of relief no closer to the hole.

Correction: Place a tee at the nearest point not closer to the hole, measure one club length, and drop the ball from shoulder height.

RELIEF FROM AN IMMOVABLE OBSTRUCTION

The right foot is resting on a sprinkler head, which is an immovable obstruction. Relief is allowed if it interferes with the stance or swing.

FOOTPRINTS/IMMOVABLE AND MOVABLE OBSTRUCTIONS

The ball is in a footprint. Relief is not allowed. The objects on the left of the ball are movable obstructions: a rake, a pencil, a cup, and an empty golf ball sleeve. If they interfere with the stance or swing in a hazard the player may remove them. Objects on the right are loose impediments: a stone, a stick, a pine cone, and a leaf. If any of these are in a hazard and interfere with the player's stance or swing, he or she is not allowed relief or permitted to move them.

INTERFERENCE

Both the tree and the 150-yard marker interfere with the backswing. There is no relief from the tree, but there is relief from the marker.

It's obvious that the marker is going to interfere with the backswing. But relief is not allowed because the stake is actually a movable obstruction.

Remove the stake, which is placed in a PVC pipe sleeve, and play the shot as the ball lies. If the stake is imbedded in the ground or in concrete it is an immovable obstruction. Find the nearest point not closer to the hole where the stake would not interfere with your backswing, measure one club length, and drop the ball.

7

TIPS FOR THE SMART GOLFER

The term "course management" has come into vogue the past few years, replacing "playing smart" or "playing stupid"—although the latter phrases are more descriptive. What has to be managed? Two things—judgment and emotions. Course management includes psychological control as well as strategy.

There are a growing number of golf specialists who deal solely in the field of psychology. This book will only touch lightly on the psychological aspects of golf; for a more in-depth treatment of this subject, read *The New Golf Mind*, which I wrote with Dr. Richard Coop.*

Believe in yourself as a golfer. Don't dwell on your shortcomings. Convince yourself you can succeed.

Fear, doubt, hesitancy, uncertainty, and indecision all lead to failure in golf.

You wouldn't be human if you didn't feel some nervousness under pressure. The champions develop strategies to reduce their fear so it doesn't keep them from performing up to their capabilities. For example: put the experience in perspective; occupy the mind with procedure to avoid dwelling on the consequences; use self hypnosis; and concentrate on images of past successes.

Anger is a self-defeating response in golf if it produces muscular tension and reduces the ability to think rationally. It can be useful; but golfers normally should maintain an inner calm and not become angry.

Strategy, tactics, and smart play are a part of course management. Although I'm a long hitter, I've taken my share of drubbings from players

---

*Wiren, Gary, and Richard Coop. *The New Golf Mind*. New York: Simon & Shuster, 1978.

149

whose drives I've surpassed by 25 to 50 yards, so I can personally attest to the superior wisdom of being a smart player rather than a long hitter.

Playing smart means:

1. Not automatically using a driver because the hole is a par four or par five. Some holes call for a shorter tee shot to be safe or a particularly straight tee shot that is difficult with a driver.

2. Selecting a club that allows you to make a comfortable swing.

3. Choosing a club with less loft for playing into the wind, uphill, and for intentionally slicing; and choosing one with more loft for playing with the wind, downhill, and for intentionally hooking.

4. Playing to the safe part of the green when the pin is in a precarious place that allows little margin of error.

5. Teeing the ball close to the trouble so you can hit away from it.

6. Not pressing for extra distance when playing into a stiff wind.

Playing golf intelligently, using the best odds and least risk, will reduce your number of "disaster" holes. You don't have to be smart to play smart golf; you have to be sensible. I would bet that Jack Nicklaus uses his 3-wood from the tee instead of his driver more often than any other modern PGA Tour player. I'd say he's a pretty smart golfer.

MARKING YOUR DISTANCE

On par-3 holes check the permanent marker for the distance to the center of the green. The tee markers may be several yards ahead or behind the distance marker. Walk off the distance from the blocks to the permanent marker to determine your distance to the green.

PRESSING FOR DISTANCE

Mistake: On long holes such as this 463-yard par 4, don't strain for extra distance. The effort will only create tension, which destroys a good swing motion.

Correction: Make your normal effort and your best swing. Don't press for long holes and long hitters.

TEEING UP THE BALL NEAR A WATER HAZARD

Mistake: The ball is teed up on the wrong side. This encourages the player to aim toward the water hazard.

Correction: Tee the ball up closer to the hazard and drive the ball away from the trouble, not toward it.

CHIPPING OUT OF TROUBLE

Mistake: When chipping out of trouble from loose dirt, loose sand, or pine needles, don't position the ball too far forward.

The resulting swing will hit behind the ball and move it only a few feet forward.

Correction: Play the ball back toward the right foot with a club of about a 7-iron loft. From this position there is less chance of hitting the ground first.

PREPARING FOR COMPETITION

A player in competition should be prepared for all eventualities. Towels, extra gloves, and umbrella are critical: if a player can't keep the grips dry, he or she will lose total control of the club. The extra shoes help if there are 36 holes to play or if the tournament lasts more than one day.

Some of the equipment necessary for playing in cold weather: a good rain suit, extra sweaters, an extra pair of socks, extra gloves, and a hat.

DEVELOPING A ROUTINE FOR CONSISTENCY

Consistency is an absolutely necessary skill for a golfer. It begins with developing a routine. Here is a complete routine, from start to finish.

Assess the lie to determine club selection and the type of shot.

Determine the yardage to the flag or to whatever location you intend to play. This may be done with a yardage book, a scorecard, or notes you've taken previously. And, of course, it can be done visually.

Also check the wind to help in club selection and the type of shot.

Visualize the shot. This is a very important part of making consistent golf shots. See it *before* you do it.

Select a club.   Aim from behind, drawing an imaginary
                                            line from the flag to the ball, and
                                            approach from the rear.

Grip the club and assess the distance from the ball by measuring with your left arm against your chest and walking into the shot.

Sole the club, feeling your left arm on your chest.

While taking the address position, stay in motion with a waggle or two—don't let tension build up in the body.

Swing to the top.

Swing to the finish.

Evaluate the result. If it was good, savor it and imprint it in your memory. If it was poor, take a practice swing the way it should have been and visualize the desired result.

8

A FINAL WORD OF ADVICE:
VISUALIZATION

Visual study is an effective way to enhance learning and performance in a motor skill like golf. Review the pictures in this book, compare them with others in golf magazines and books, then look at yourself in a mirror or on video or in photos.

Share your information and thoughts with your golf professional so that you have a trained, objective eye to help you sort out the correct from the incorrect. It will help make your game easier and your scores lower.

Gary Wiren

APPENDIX:
THE RULES OF GOLF

Do you know of any other game with 18 million participants (in the United States alone) in which less than one percent know the rules, contained in a book of a little over 120 pages? It's not that the rules are simple; they couldn't be and cover all the variables of play on 15,000 different courses. But the fact is that most golfers have never read the rule book, although it is available in almost any golf shop.

The rules provide conditions under which players may compete fairly. They are meant to be equitable, not punitive. No player should be allowed an advantage over another except by skill. When the rules don't cover a situation, fairness should prevail.

The original thirteen rules didn't cover every situation—today there are thirty-four plus a substantial appendix.

And that's not all: the rules-making bodies, the United States Golf Association and the Royal and Ancient Golf Club of St. Andrews, publish a book of decisions that challenges the thickness of an unabridged dictionary. This book chronicles the individual cases over the years that led to the establishment and changes in the rules.

Buy a copy of the rule book and read four pages a night for a month. You can finish the entire text and the index in a single 31-day period. By doing so, you will join a very select company in the world of golf—those who have read the rules. (Note: a two-page etiquette section precedes the rules; from what I've seen on the course, it hasn't been widely read, either.)

INDEX